Rosa Loves to Read

Written by Diane Z. Shore

Illustrated by Larry Day

Children's Press®
A Division of Scholastic Inc.
New York • Toronto • London • Auckland • Sydney
Mexico City • New Delhi • Hong Kong
Danbury, Connecticut

To Jenn, who loves to read
—D.S.

Reading Consultants

Linda Cornwell
Literacy Specialist

Katharine A. Kane
Education Consultant
(Retired, San Diego County Office of Education
and San Diego State University)

Library of Congress Cataloging-in-Publication Data

Shore, Diane ZuHone.
  Rosa loves to read / written by Diane Shore ; illustrated by Larry Day.
      p. cm. — (Rookie reader)
  Summary: Rosa loves to read when everything is quiet.
   ISBN 0-516-21723-2 (lib. bdg.)   0-516-25825-7 (pbk.)
   [1. Books and reading—Fiction. 2. Noise—Fiction.] I. Day, Larry, 1956- ill.
   II. Title. III. Series.
   PZ7.S558672Ro 2003
   [E]–dc21
                              2003007119

CHILDREN'S PRESS, and A ROOKIE READER®, and associated logos are trademarks
and or registered trademarks of Scholastic Library Publishing. SCHOLASTIC and
associated logos are trademarks and or registered trademarks of Scholastic Inc.
7 8 9 10 11 12 R 14 13 12 11 10 09   62

Dogs bark.

Feet stomp.

Rosa tries to read.

Horns honk.
Balloons pop.

Rosa tries to read.

Rosa yells, "QUIET!"

Toes tiptoe.
Cats purr.

Rosa turns the page.

Motors hum.
Spoons stir.

23

Rosa turns the page.

25

Clocks tick.
Mice squeak.

Curtains swish.
Brooms sweep.

Rosa whispers, "I love to read!"

Word List (44 words)

balloons	doors	page	sweep
balls	feet	pop	swish
bark	hands	purr	the
bounce	honk	quiet	tick
brooms	horns	read	tiptoe
cats	hum	Rosa	to
clap	I	slam	toes
clocks	lids	spoons	tries
crash	love	squeak	turns
curtains	mice	stir	whispers
dogs	motors	stomp	yells

About the Author

Diane Z. Shore is a writer and former elementary school teacher. She lives in Marietta, Georgia, with her husband, John, and their two children, Jenn and Sam (with whom she loves to read).

About the Illustrator

Larry Day lives in Illinois with his wife, Melanie, and their two sons, Andrew and Peter.